Live, Love & Laugh

21 Day Transformation to Making Better Choices

Live, Love & Laugh

21 Day Transformation to Making Better Choices

Sharilynn McIntosh

Extreme Overflow Publishing
A division of Extreme Overflow Enterprises, Inc
Grayson, Georgia 30017
www.extremeoverflow.com

Copyright ©2016 by Sharilynn McIntosh
Published by Extreme Overflow Publishing
Photography Credit: M&E Photography

Unless otherwise noted, all Scripture quotations are taken from the Life Application Study Bible, New International Version.

Manufactured in the United States of America
10 9 8 7 6 5 4 3 2 1

ISBN 978-0-9976256-6-0

INTRODUCTION

How much time do you spend regretting the
decisions you made in the past? Let me
share a secret with you. Holding onto the
past and all the negative things that you
chose to say, do and feel is NOT going
to change where you are at this moment.
So, why continue to look back? There
are so many wonderful things that you're
missing by not looking forward.

Through this book, you'll learn how
to pull out of the idle position that
you may be stuck in. You will also
learn how to look at some of the
things that impact the choices
you make, so you can move
forward to living, loving and
laughing into your purpose.
Are you ready? Let's roll!

Day 1

Do you know who you are?

_____

Your identity has a lot to do with how you make decisions. When you have a positive and healthy self-image, you can make choices clearly and concisely. Let me give you an example:

I have always had issues with my height. I am 5 feet 2 inches, and feel vertically challenged. I actually own a pair of 7 inch high heels, just so I can be seen. What I didn't realize is that I wasn't happy with what I saw in the mirror, because while I am surrounded by all types of beautiful and tall women in my family, I felt unattractive. My self-esteem was low, because I wasn't comfortable in my own skin, and that caused me to be something that I wasn't for many years. Here's what I got from that experience:

1. I am fearfully and wonderfully made (Psalm 139:14). And guess what? You are too! Think about it. If the Creator of the universe thought enough to bring you here on earth, it was for a reason. So, it's up to you to choose to tap into the fact that you are fearfully and wonderfully made.

2. I learned how to forgive myself and let go of the things that I couldn't change from my past, and so can you. When you feel guilty, angry, insecure,

inadequate and unsure, remember that you can release yourself from all those emotions by asking forgiveness from those affected by your past decisions, so that you can move forward into a new you.

Reflect and write about how you can reclaim your identity.

_____

_____

_____

_____

_____

_____

_____

_____

_____

_____

Day 2

Are you comfortable in your own skin?

_____

Do you accept who you are, flaws and all? Are you being overly critical, calling yourself names under your breath when you make a mistake? We are our own worst critics, but please don't be too hard, because nobody's perfect. That takes the pressure off when you are freed from the inner voices that say that you aren't good enough. Be responsible for your actions.

What I want you to do is to take a good, hard look at yourself, recognize what you can change, and begin to work on it, and let the rest go.

Reflect and write about how you feel in your own skin.

_____

_____

_____

_____

_____

_____

_____

_____

Day 3

Who do you
see when
you look in
the mirror?

_____

This is a deep question, because it has to do with physically, emotionally, mentally and spiritually. Where do you find yourself in this very moment? Are you living a purpose driven life, full of expectations and possibilities, or are you running away from the past mistakes? Are you marching in time, unable to move? Do you have a positive outlook on the future, and can't wait to begin anew every morning, or do you dread the sun coming up?

Do you like what you see when you look in the mirror? If you can't honestly say yes, then it's time to delve deeper so that can change.

Reflect and write about liking what you see when you look in the mirror.

_____

_____

_____

_____

_____

_____

Day 4

Are you hearing echoes of the past?

Is there someone or something from your past that keeps replaying negative messages in your head? Are you unhappy with your living situation, or regretting something you said or did that caused you to be where you are? Do you love yourself, or are you searching for someone to love you the way you feel that you need to be loved. These are thought provoking questions that you have to ask, because if the answer is no, or you're unsure about anything, then you are stuck in the past. My job is to help you to become free from the voices in your head that tell you that you're less than, or that you don't measure up. It's time for you to walk away from this place, and step into your future, which is much brighter than where you are.

Write and reflect on hearing the echoes of the past.

_____

_____

_____

_____

_____

_____

Day 5

How do you define yourself?

_____

How do you define yourself? Is your identity tied up in your career; your marriage; your children?

I spent a lot of time telling people who I was, based upon where I worked, who I was and am married to, and whose mother I am. Please understand that while you can certainly identify yourself through all of those resources, none of them is actually who you are.

What I'm talking about is your gifts and talents. Do you know what you're good at? If not, take out a pen and a piece of paper, and brainstorm. Everyone has a gift, and whether you realize it or not, you can discover what you're good at. You may only have one gift, or several. That being the case, once you have compiled your list, sit down, meditate and pray about how to find out what you're working with.

Write and reflect on how you can define yourself.

_____

_____

_____

Day 6

What have you learned from your experiences so far?

In my journey, I have learned that life is too short and precious to be unhappy and blue. I spent many years suppressing my depression. I constantly looked back, chiding myself inwardly for a lot of decisions that I certainly couldn't change. I had to look in the mirror, and do some real soul searching. You can relive every bad choice that you made, but for what? Yes, there are some lessons that you needed to learn, so that you don't repeat any mistakes, but to continue to beat yourself up over things that you can't rewrite in your history is pointless, and wastes a lot of time.

What I did, and continue to do for peace of mind and sanity is to repent and ask for forgiveness from God, and anyone else who was impacted as a result of my behavior, actions or decisions that I made. Secondly, and this is the hardest part; I have forgiven myself and CHOOSE to walk in healing and wholeness. Now let me give a disclaimer right here, because I don't want anyone to think that I have arrived. No one ever arrives, because there are varying degrees of healing. Wholeness is the end result, but there is a journey, and everyone has to walk it. So, the choice is yours. Are you ready to run your race? I'm here to help. On your mark, get set, go!

Write and reflect on what you have learned from the past.

_____

_____

_____

_____

_____

_____

_____

_____

_____

_____

_____

_____

_____

_____

_____

Day 7

When do you start?

There are plenty of ways to ask that question, but it takes insight, prayer and a lot of willpower. Don't put off tomorrow what you can do today, so just get to it. Procrastination is a time killer, and you can't stop time from moving, so it's better to try and fail, so you can start again than to just not do it for fear of failure. No other way to put it.

This is the question that has most people frozen in their steps. A lot of it has to do with feelings of fear and inadequacy, or being concerned about what others may think. The bottom line is that everyone deserves to experience happiness in their lifetime. However, keep in mind that happiness is a temporary state of mind, which fades, but joy lasts forever. That sounded too easy, right? Not really, because joy will keep a smile on your face when all hell is breaking loose in your life. Joy will have you smiling through the tears, because you know a better day is coming. This is what you want to look forward to. Change may be frightening, but very necessary. Look at it this way; there are plenty of people who have been where you are, and felt the way you feel. They may have fallen many a time, but got back up and tried it again, and eventually was successful, and they didn't look back at the failures, but looked toward the triumphs. So can you. Feel the fear, and do it anyway, and you will see the results of overcoming trepidation and running into your future.

Write and reflect on how to begin again.

_____

_____

_____

_____

_____

_____

_____

_____

_____

_____

_____

_____

Day 8

What's love got to do with it?

———————————

Women know how to put on a mask. Makeup is flawless at all times. However women can look gorgeous on the outside, but be broken on the inside. I know, because I did it for years. I became a master of smiling through the tears, afraid of showing people who I really am.

I hid my fears of being unloved due to feelings of rejection and low self-esteem. Ever hear of the term "looking for love in all the wrong places, and in too many faces?" That was me; searching for love in sources that couldn't possibly complete me.

In the Bible, John 3:16 says that God loved mankind so much that He gave His one and only Son to save the world. That is the ultimate display of love, to lay down your life for someone who can't possibly understand or imagine why.

I had a hard time accepting God's love, but once I did, it was a stepping stone to other avenues of love that I needed to explore. I had to learn how to love myself and others. Let's face it; everyone isn't going to like or love you. There are enemies or haters that aren't interested in your wellbeing. At the end of the day, learn how to love yourselves, so you can love everyone else.

Write and reflect on how to love and accept yourself.

_____

_____

_____

_____

_____

_____

_____

_____

_____

_____

_____

_____

Day 9

Will I ever fall in love again?

Have you ever felt like you'll never love again? As a child, there was that cute individual that caught your eye. You went out of your way to get their attention, only to be broken hearted by the feelings not being reciprocated.

You may have thought that there something was wrong with you, or that something was wrong with them. Please understand that neither is the case. You were young, and had no clue about what love was in a relationship.

Unfortunately, you may still feel that way with regards to a lack of a love interest, or a failed relationship.

Reflect and write about not falling in love again.

Day 10

Do you have real friends?

_____

It's better to be surrounded by a few friends that will love you enough to tell you the truth about yourself, rather than strangers and acquaintances who will tell you how great you are. People who really care about you are your true friends. They will not allow you to make a fool of yourself. They will lovingly express their apprehensions about something or someone that you may not see or feel is wrong for you. True friends will never betray your confidences. A true friend will never throw you under the bus, or broadcast your business on the 11:00 news.

Do you have any true friends?

Reflect and write about what friendship means to you.

_____

_____

_____

_____

_____

_____

Day 11

Should you guard your heart?

_____

Your heart is a valuable instrument within your body. While your heart is strong, it's fragile at the same time and for this reason, it is important that you protect your heart.

Some of the ways you can protect your heart is to make sure that it's clean. To have a clean heart means to be free of bitterness, rage and anger. Protecting your heart also means forgiveness. Forgiveness is for you, even if people never apologize.

Protecting your heart allows you to be free to love others. Don't be afraid to love again after being hurt. God will remove the hurt and restore your trust in being able to love again.

Sometimes it's better to love from a distance, and that's ok. Unhealthy relationships can break your heart if you don't allow God to heal it.

Reflect and write about how you may need to guard your heart.

_____

_____

_____

Day 12

Is it time to prioritize your love and put it in perspective?

Love is one of the most powerful emotions a person can experience. There are various types of love. Love for God, love for self, love for significant others, love for children, love for family and friends, and love for mankind.

God is love. His very nature is loving. He loves us unconditionally, but it's important for you to love yourself. If you choose not to love yourself, it will be hard for others to love you. When you exhaust the value of love seen in your everyday life, others will do the same as you establish boundaries.

Reflect and write about ways that you can love yourself to a healthy place.

_____

_____

_____

_____

_____

_____

_____

Day 13

Have you
found yourself
in the dog
parlor?

_____

This is my shout out to all the singles. I want to leave something with you to think about. What attracts you to a certain person? Is it looks? Personality? Bank account? The car they drive? The house they have? A great looking body?

The sum of a person's parts doesn't necessarily make them whole. You can be drop dead gorgeous, yet be lacking in compassion. They may have a large bank account, and an obese mansion, but they are hooked on phonics, or even worse.

If you're a woman who is attracted to the bad boy image, know that you most likely are setting yourself up for failure. If you're a man that wants a woman to fulfill your sexual fantasy like a pole stripper, you're probably not the only one that feels that way.

Take a closer look. Who you attract all has to do with your self-esteem. Think about it? What is attractive about a roughneck or a stripper? Do they speak to your intellect? Do they share your value system? Or is it the danger that makes you curious, like the attraction two people have in the movies? At the end of the day, you want to view a potential mate as someone who can be a spouse as well as a parent, value someone with integrity, who will love wholeheartedly, even with flaws. Be careful not to invite unnecessary drama into your life. Don't forget to guard your heart. Value yourself enough to know that you deserve the best. If the roughneck or stripper isn't the best thing, then reach for the stars. Pray for the right person to come into your life, and then inspect their fruit. You will know who they are by how they treat others. The choice is yours.

Reflect and write about attractions.

_____

_____

_____

_____

_____

_____

_____

_____

_____

Day 14

Are you ready to saddle up?

_____

You may have been hurt and betrayed by those who said they loved you. One thing to keep in mind is that there is only one who loves unconditionally, and that is God. The rest are flawed human beings, capable of making mistakes.

If you find yourself holding on to feelings of inadequacy, guilt or shame as the result of being hurt by someone, be careful that you don't allow your heart to be hardened, so you can love again.

Write and reflect on how to love again after being hurt.

_____

_____

_____

_____

_____

_____

_____

_____

Day 15

When's the last time you had a little comedic relief?

_____

Take a moment out of your day to find the humor in life. Don't take yourself so seriously that you forget how to smile. One of my favorite TV shows was a comedy that displayed the cast making mistakes, going off script, and doing everything they could not to laugh.

Sometimes it can't be helped. It takes more muscles to frown than it does to smile. So, the next time you're feeling down, turn on the TV and look at something that will make you fall on the floor laughing and in tears.

Write and reflect on laughter.

_____

_____

_____

_____

_____

_____

_____

Day 16

What's so funny?

_____

With all the pressure of life, you have to stop and look at something that will make you laugh. Life is entirely too short not to appreciate humor.

Think back to your childhood. Is there anything that you recall saying or doing that will bring a smile to your face? If not, ask your parents or siblings? Take out your picture album, and show it to your spouse and children, and recollect the good old days, when life was simpler.

I recently had a conversation with one of my sisters, and she reminded me of something I said as a child that was long forgotten. She and my other sister busted out laughing when I repeated the phrase. I had to laugh, because while I'm a completely different person as an adult, I had to admit how silly I was as a kid.

My suggestion is to take time each day, and laugh. The Bible reminds us that laughter is a good medicine for what ails us. Try it!

Write and reflect on fun childhood memories.

Day 17

What's your reason to smile?

_____

Those who have experienced bullying know all too well how it feels to be laughed at. It's not funny to be ridiculed. People who fall on the floor in laughter after someone trips understand what I mean.

Everyone isn't part of the culture of cool kids. The general population isn't an actor, entertainer or model. For many years, I didn't feel that I was attractive, and that I gave birth to the most beautiful children on the planet. I was a geek, and I worked hard to get an education.

There was a lot of time doing silly things in order to get noticed and to fit in. It took a long time for people to take me seriously as an adult, because of what I did as a kid and during those oh so awkward teenage years.

Even as a young adult, there were those who talked to me a certain way, or took advantage of me because of my world view at the time. However, once I started to really mature into who I am today, those people were quickly cut out of my life, and I surrounded myself with real friends.

Finally, I learned how not to take myself so seriously, and laugh with others who knew how to have fun. The only thing that I get teased about nowadays is my extremely thick Boston accent.

Write and reflect about acceptance of yourself versus fitting in.

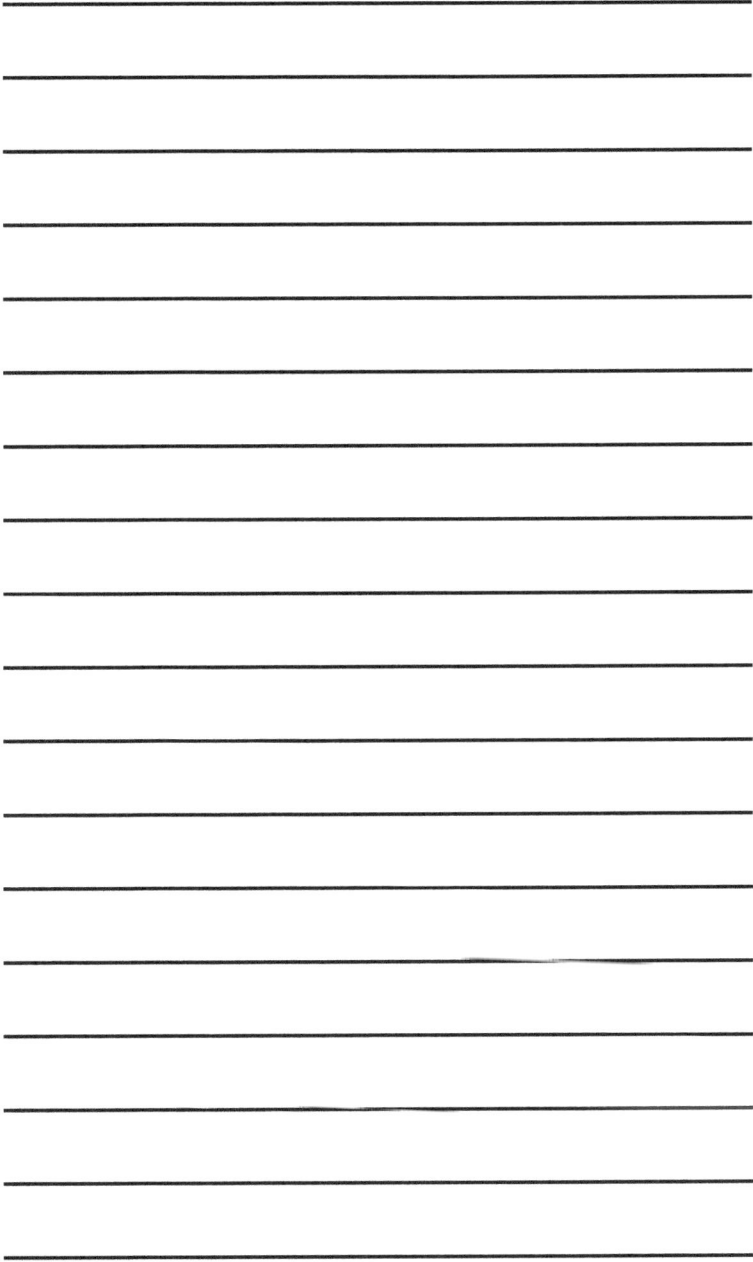

Day 18

When was the last time you changed your style?

_____

With every new morning there is also a new beginning, even if it means reforming a former moment. Take a look at fashion and music for an example. The things that were once worn back in the 50's and 60's are still being worn today. The music that made no sense to our parents when we were listening and dancing to it is being sampled in our children's music lyrics today. I bet if you look at some throwback pictures, you will think about a song and remember how your neighborhood looked at that period in time, and what was popular in fashion and have a great time reminiscing!

Don't laugh too hard, but on the left is me at age 17, and on the right is me present day. My hair and makeup are different, but I'm still enjoying life!

For today's entry, pull that favorite outfit from the back of the closet (if you still have it), take out your records, dust them off, and party like its 1999!

Reflect and write about how your style has changed through the years. Create a fresh look and mark a new beginning.

_____

_____

_____

_____

_____

_____

_____

_____

_____

_____

_____

Day 19

Have you tapped into real joy?

_____

Have you ever heard the saying that happiness is temporary, but joy is eternal? Let me elaborate by saying that happiness comes with circumstances. If all is well, you may be happy. But joy stays when happiness gets up and leaves.

Joy is a permanent condition that causes you to smile when all hell is breaking loose in your life. When you have absolutely nothing to be happy about, joy will remind you of the brighter day. Nothing lasts forever, and even though you might be going through something, a change will inevitably occur in your life.

After the rain, the sun comes out, right? No matter what season it is, you will encounter a bright sunny day. Those are the times that most people live for. It doesn't have to be gloom and doom when it's cloudy outside, or a storm is looming nearby. Learn how to laugh in the rain and snow.

I remember when my youngest daughter would love to run outside and play in the rain. She wore an expression of sheer delight as she jumped through the puddles. That's what we need to do! For the fun of it, the next time it rains, put on your waterproof gear and run outside. You may be surprised at who will join you.

Reflect and write about a time when you experienced the greatest joy.

_____

_____

_____

_____

_____

_____

_____

_____

_____

_____

_____

_____

Day 20

Have you
lost your
smile?

_____

There are going to be times in life when circumstances won't make you happy, and the tears will fall. People may try to make you laugh, but it's not working, and the cloud of gloom and doom stays over your head.

I'm not saying that this doesn't happen, but you have to reach down inside and grab all of your resources, whether it's your faith, past events, or just taking time out to go for a walk.

If you look at life through the eyes of a child, you will find out their worldview. They may be sad for a moment, but they shake it off, and find joy in something else. Kids are great for moving on, no matter what life throws at them, especially if they're seven and under.

Why not be childlike for a moment. Look at your favorite kids show. I find that Sesame Street and the Muppets do it for me, but can't wait to get tickets for the movie featuring my favorite character, Snoopy!

Reflect and write about a happy time in your childhood that makes you smile.

Day 21

What is your
happiest
memory?

The Christmas season has always been my favorite time of year. While I am a Christian, and my faith is certainly grounded in the story of Jesus' birth, the kid in me has always found something peaceful and magical at the same time about the lights, decorations and snow.

This is the only time of year that I don't mind having a coat on, and my mind goes back to when I used to look out of the window at 3:00 in the morning, looking for Santa's sleigh. I love everything about it, from the shopping to the music, although I feel that it's a bit commercialized, but I enjoy it, nonetheless.

If you don't have any children, look at your relatives and find the smiles on your nieces, nephews and cousins when they open up their gifts. Say a silent prayer, and embrace that moment of the wide eyed wonder. Everybody becomes a kid at Christmas, because of the fun memories.

Take in the sights, smells and sounds of the season. Sing your favorite Christmas songs. Go outside and make a snow angel. Have a snowball fight. Build a snowman and a fort. Stick out your tongue and taste a snowflake. Build a fire, make some S'mores and drink hot chocolate or egg nog. Take a picture with Santa to the surprise of the other adults and kids watching you. Have some fun, and most of all, don't forget to live in the moment, love deeply, and laugh hysterically!

Write and reflect about your favorite Christmas memory as a child.

_____

_____

_____

_____

_____

_____

_____

_____

_____

_____

_____

ACKNOWLEDGEMENTS

I would like to take this opportunity to thank Extreme Overflow Publishing, which has an amazing brand and writing coaching specialty. I appreciate all that they have poured into me. They worked tirelessly, and helped me to realize my dreams with regards to encouraging others to make better choices and move forward. I appreciate their special gift of making the ordinary come to life.

My support system of family, friends and church family that keep me grounded and accountable for all that I say and do. I wouldn't be able to share my personal experiences if I hadn't gone through them. Trust me, I haven't arrived, but I certainly have grown a lot from my mistakes, and hope that you will too. Thank you all for your support!

www.ingramcontent.com/pod-product-compliance
Lightning Source LLC
Chambersburg PA
CBHW060357050426

42449CB00009B/1781